Assume Nothing
by Leanne Franson

SLAB-O CONCRETE

Bibliography

Impeccable Taste is a new version of **The Fagless Fag-Hag** (*Liliane Minicomics #2 – #5*) for the anthology *The First Time: True Stories, Volume 2*.
(Charles Montpetit, editor, 1995 Ocra Book Publishers, Victoria, Canada, ISBN 1 55143 039 8)

Loose Skin fist appeared around 1992 as **Liliane Minicomics #9**
(Leanne Franson, Montreal, Canada, ISSN 1201 3552)

Proximal Possibilities, Of Dating And Dogs and **Mixed Blessings** were first published in **OH... a comic quarterly for her, because it's time** in May, August and November 1993 respectively.
(Hope, editor, B Publications, Victoria, Canada, ISSN 1192 4047)

Flicks And Finales appears here for the first time. It was written for **OH... #6** but this was withheld by the author after 'Mixed Blessings' was published alongside a pro-censorship editorial preface in *OH... #5*.

Breeders first appeared in **Dyke's Delight #2**
(Kate Charlesworth, editor, Fanny, publisher ISBN 0 86166 111 7)

Do It Myself appears here for the first time.

Breeders Too was created for this collection.

Orca Book Publishers: Box 5626, Station B, Victoria, BC, V8R 6S4, Canada
B Publications: PO Box 41030, 5134 Cordova Bay Rd, Victoria, BC, V8Y 2K0, Canada
Liliane: PO Box 274, Succ. Place du Parc, Montreal, Quebec, H2W 2N8, Canada
Fanny: c/o Knockabout, 10 Acklam Rd, London, W10 5QZ, UK

About the artist

Leanne Franson started drawing comics in 1986 when she caught Fineartophobia after finishing her Studio Art degree. Seeking her escape in newspaper comics, she quickly became convinced her life was funnier than that of *Garfield* and *Cathy*.

Now that she's actually earning a living with her illustration skills she finds it harder to pump out issues of her minicomic *Liliane* but has managed to squeeze in time to do new material for this collection. Hope you've enjoyed it.

Her work has also appeared in such titles as *Dyke Strippers, Action Girl Comics, Black Sheets, GirlFrenzy, Men Are From Detroit – Women Are From Paris, Gay Comics, Strange Looking Exile, GirlJock, What Is This Thing Called Sex?* as well as more than thirty issues of her own *Liliane Minicomics*. Write to Leanne at PO Box 274, Succ. Place du Parc, Montreal, Que, H2W 2N8, Canada or Slab-O-Concrete for more information. Please go out and pick up independent and self-published comics and zines. There is so much under-appreciated talent out there.

Acknowledgements: Special thanks to Peter Pavement, Steve Marchant, Charles Monpetit, Roz Warren, my Mom, and everyone else who has encouraged me, written to me, and bought my work.

A big nod to Larry-Bob's **Queer Zine Explosion** disclaimer: "Nothing should be assumed about anybody's sexuality, including yours," for inspiring this book's title. Get yourself a copy of *Queer Zine Explosion*, a directory of queer orientated underground media, by sending postage to Box 591275, San Francisco, CA, 94159-1275, USA.

Assume Nothing

Third Printing 1999, (first and second printings 1997)

Published by Slab-O-Concrete Publications
PO Box 148, Hove, BN3 3DQ, UK
mail@slab-o-concrete.demon.co.uk

ISBN 1 899866 04 3

Printed in Canada by Hignell Book Printing Ltd

Mona wasn't much comfort...

That's men for you.

... and then i lost her too!

... i got accepted at the University of Toronto this fall!!

That September i was a pitiful sight indeed.

... no fag friend, no room-mate... what am i gonna do?

Then one day i bumped into one of Mona's friends:

... hiya liliane! You look a bit down!... miss Mona, eh... well, come with me to the women's center if you're not busy right now...

Feeling too apathetic to refuse...

... god, i'll never live this down if Mona finds out!

You'll love the women's center!

... i tagged along...

... oh my god!! ... a feminist hell-hole!

⑦

(16)

I never did get a chance to try out my practiced-on-my-hand technique with Mikki...

...now WHY did i think lesbians would be better for my sex life than gay men?...

...in fact we never even kissed again.

My love and desire for her didn't die quickly...

O ...maybe if i write and tell her how i feel, she'll...

... although i eventually moved on.

2nd Anniversary!!
liliane and Sophie

But back then i discovered...

...you look a bit down, liliane...

...that my taste in love objects was still... impeccable.

I'm in love with Mikki...

...yeah, me too! ...but she's in love with Millie.

Loose Skin in old montréal
OR in other words: epidermis anonymous erraticus

one year i moved into Old Montréal... MÉTRO SQUARE VICTORIA

With a reputation for being picturesque

it was inhabited by a clockwork set of zombies...

...who fled at nightfall by public transport to continue their lifeless lives elsewhere...

...leaving an eerily empty void of institutional monuments...

1883

...where the sparce populace of illicit artsies presaged the area's future "lofty" status...

①

...no small feat considering the only running water was in the "public washroom" down the hall...

...shared with 5 other starving artists "working" on my floor. ④

Soon, however, i moved my futon out of the tent and into my one "clean" room.

The presence of the $50 fridge and the stuffed animals on the bed helped convince the Bell man to give me a residential line.

FRIDGE

Ensconsed in the smell of fresh paint

i thoroughly enjoyed my vaguely macabre location

13 Girlhood tales of Laura Ingalls Wilder evoked the inspirational recollection of salt-cured pork...

SALT PORK

PICKLES 2 for 1¢

...Surely it couldn't be too complex, even in these modern urban times.

520g

So, i heavily salted my prize and wrapped it well in wax paper.

SIFTO

When the salt became damp i changed the wrappings.

The fatty subcutaneous layer insisted on rendering my wax paper oily, so i replaced it with reynolds wrap.

...the taxidermists being less than helpful (they wanted for me to bring in my "animal" for treatment) ... i headed for the public library...

TO BE CONTINUED...

In any case, i swore i'd deliver a grandchild to Mom before i was 25...

OVERLY NAIVE AND OPTIMISTIC 22-YEAR OLD QUALIFIED TO WORK IN COUNTER-SERVICE CAFÉS

DIPLOMA WITH $8000 owing

Now that i've got my ARTS DEGREE i'll be rich and famous... i'll be able to afford a baby within the next three years, no problem!!

...which was soon revised to "before i'm thirty":

But i'm already thirty!!

TIME

I was EIGHT YEARS OLD When my Mom was 30!!!

I seldom actually considered How to get my 'baby'... in fact at 17 i had a real scare:

...i'm sorry MS. FRANSON... you'll have to come back in for a second urine test... it was too early in the cycle for conclusive results...

Just out of high school, still 'straight', and using the "withdrawal method" with Catholic boyfriend

When i was younger, more effort was spent avoiding pregnancy than working towards it...

...let's see... the pill won't kick in for another two weeks, so we can use condoms ...or i'll try to get him to use condoms...

...i should back up anything with nonoxynol-9 spermicide foam

Later, with women, i discovered the pleasures of NOT anxiously awaiting each period:

I'm FREE!!!

(note: pre-safer-sex-with-lesbians-too)

I finally settled down... with a lovely lady as family-oriented as me:

...well, i hope you make nice babies together...

...Mom! I'm in love!! And SHE wants kids too!!!

②

ANOTHER MASSOTHERAPEUTE LOSES THAT LOVING FEELING.

BREEDERS TOO ... reprise of a theme ...

Well, 30 has graciously come and gone...

...and my potential fellow-mommy too...

But not the desire to join the **BREEDER** ranks...

Now, avowedly single, i forged ahead in my parental plans...